ESTHER
For such a time as this

Joy Dass

short course

The way of
THE SPIRIT
resources@thewayofthespirit.com
www.thewayofthespirit.com

Published in Great Britain by The Way of The Spirit, Norfolk, UK
www.thewayofthespirit.com

First edition published September 2023

The Way of The Spirit is a charity registered in England and Wales, number
1110648

ISBN 978-1-9085-2868-1

Contents

The Way of The Spirit Bible reading course   i

How to use this booklet   ii

Introduction   1

Esther Chapter One   4

Esther Chapter Two   8

Esther Chapter Three   14

Esther Chapter Four   19

Esther Chapters Five and Six   25

Esther Chapter Seven   31

Esther Chapters Eight to Nine   36

Conclusion   41

Appendix   47

Going deeper   50

ESTHER
For such a time as this

THE WAY OF THE SPIRIT BIBLE READING COURSE

The purpose of this short course and the recorded teaching that goes with it is partly to give you some impression of how The Way of The Spirit Bible Reading Course works. It is not, however, just an excerpt or collection of excerpts from the fuller course, but a properly integrated short course in its own right, and as such is somewhat different in presentation.

- The full course takes you systematically through the whole Bible, chapter by chapter, with the help of a textbook; here you have only a little booklet giving a brief survey of a Bible theme.

- The full course has more comprehensive worksheets.

- The full course recordings offer more systematic teaching arranged in twenty-minute parts.

Nevertheless, by using these materials you should capture the flavour of the full course quite well. The purpose of The Way of The Spirit is to help Christians tap into the life that is to be found in the Bible and the power of the Spirit revealed in its pages, to help you understand what the Bible is all about, what the way of God's Spirit is in it, and how to enter more fully into the richness of life men of Bible-times enjoyed. You should find all these aims met in some measure as you use this booklet.

ESTHER
For such a time as this

If after completing this short study you wish to proceed to the fuller course, please e-mail us at resources@thewayofthespirit.com or visit our website at **www.thewayofthespirit.com**

May God bless you richly as you study his Word.

Hᴏᴡ ᴛᴏ ᴜsᴇ ᴛʜɪs ʙᴏᴏᴋʟᴇᴛ

This booklet is arranged in eight sections that will take you through the book of Esther. Each section contains written notes and some questions. The notes will help you to focus on the central themes of the story, and the questions will help you determine what you have learned, and encourage you to apply that in practical living.

It is recommended that you read through the book of Esther whilst completing this short course, as there are many references to the biblical narrative that will be much clearer having read the story for yourself. This course is designed to take you back to scripture and is no substitute for it.

As such you can use this short course by itself with your Bible, or by studying in a small group. Experience has shown that group study is much more fruitful.

A series of talks by the author on the book of Esther is available on our website at no charge. You may find it

helpful to listen to the recordings for background
information, but they are optional and not required
for this study. [1]

The recommended method of study is:

1.   Read the passage in Esther corresponding to the
     section of notes you are about to use.

2.   Read the passages at the head of the questions
     (if different). Now referring back to the booklet
     as required, answer all the questions.

3.   Write down your answers, as briefly as possible,
     using only a few words, or at most a couple of
     sentences each time. As you do so, pray the Lord
     will show you how your reading and answers
     are to relate to your own life as a Christian.

4.   If you discuss the readings in a group, try to
     stick to the set themes. It is so easy to go off at
     tangents, consider many interesting topics, and
     in the end miss the whole purpose of the study.
     The questions are to help you avoid doing that,
     by keeping your thoughts directed to the
     important, central issues.

5.   In a group, do not hurry the study. Its purpose is
     to help you grow spiritually as well as in

---

[1] To listen to or download the recordings go to our website at
www.thewayofthespirit.com/audio and search for *Esther – for such a time as
this*.

understanding, and that takes prayer as well as reading.

6. If you are using the course in a group, discuss your answers to the questions, share your insights and encourage one another to grow in the Lord. Remember to allow time for prayer and fellowship as well.

Whichever method you choose, learn to listen for what the Holy Spirit has to tell you—about your beliefs, attitudes and lifestyle. Ask yourself what lessons you should be learning from your readings, so that you can apply them to your own understanding and life as a Christian.

ESTHER
For such a time as this

For such a time as this . . .

. . . divine purpose despite natural circumstances

ESTHER
For such a time as this

ESTHER

FOR SUCH A TIME AS THIS

INTRODUCTION

Out of this book, where there is no explicit reference to his name, God speaks

Remarkably, there is no mention of God in the book of Esther, though it is unarguable that within this story we learn of the sovereign hand of God. We see his power at work to deliver those set apart for himself: securing a remnant as he did at the time of Jacob,[2] as he did in carrying his people out of Egypt, and as he did in the desert years.

Out of this book, where there is no explicit reference to his name, God speaks.

This is what the LORD says to his anointed,
to Cyrus, whose right hand I take hold of
to subdue nations before him
and to strip kings of their armour,
to open doors before him
so that gates will not be shut:
I will go before you
and will level the mountains;
I will break down gates of bronze

---

[2] Genesis 45:7

ESTHER
For such a time as this

and cut through bars of iron.
I will give you hidden treasures,
riches stored in secret places,
so that you may know that I am the LORD,
the God of Israel, who summons you by name.

(Isaiah 45:1-3)

Cyrus the Great was the founder of the first Persian empire and is mentioned multiple times in the Old Testament. This pagan king was to be used for God's purposes, as prophesied through Isaiah some 150 years before his birth. The Jews had been in exile a long time, held captive by the Babylonians. The news of this great king Cyrus advancing from the east filled them with hope of liberation. Could this pagan king be God's instrument to free the exiles and allow them to return to their homeland?

Though Cyrus himself did not acknowledge the God of Israel, he respected the beliefs and customs of the people. In the first year of his reign, he issued a proclamation allowing the exiles to return to Jerusalem and rebuild the temple, destroyed by the Babylonians. Some 50,000 returned.

From the return of the exiles to the completion of the temple, the Jews faced much opposition. It took 20 years, during the reign of Cyrus and later Darius, for the temple to be completed. The people living around Jerusalem at that time incited fear with battle threats to halt the building work the Jews had begun. God used the prophets Haggai and Zechariah to motivate the Jews to restart the work, which flourished under the prophetic word and was completed around 516 BC.

The Persian empire grew in influence and dominion through successive kings. Xerxes, king of Persia from 486-465BC, ruled half the world of that time, his empire divided up under the leadership of local governors or satraps. His kingdom covered a vast expanse, from India in the West to Cush (Ethiopia) in the east. His residence in Susa—also known as Shushan—was one of the central capitals of Persia. (Photographs appear in archaeological records; the area is now a world heritage site).

In those days the Jews were scattered widely across the vast Persian empire. As a people, they were distinct and different, adhering to their strict religious practices as outlined in the Mosaic law.

Just decades after the completion of the temple in Jerusalem, the Jewish people were about to face yet another threat . . .

ESTHER CHAPTER ONE

The king's call

---

*Consequences
always follow
disobedience to
authority*

The banquet gathering of nobles, officials and military leaders, perhaps like a modern-day summit, is the opening scene to the book of Esther. Such occasions offered opportunity for rulers of the day to demonstrate their influence, power and vast wealth. The powerful King Xerxes was pleased to display the riches of his kingdom, his splendour and glory. The royal wine flowed freely.

Xerxes' queen, Vashti, was the most important woman in the kingdom. Amongst the women of the harem, it was Vashti who would be present at official engagements. She was there to do the king's bidding, as were all the other women, set apart for the king alone. So the king called for Vashti, for she was beautiful to behold.

It is not clear why Vashti refused to come before the king when summoned. Perhaps the fact that he was in 'high spirits' rendered the invitation unappealing—or did she consider that her position gave her the right to do so?

Whatever Vashti's reason, her refusal cost her the throne and her access to, and relationship with, the king. The king's advisers made the political and social impact very clear. Assertion by Vashti of her own will could cause a rebellion throughout the kingdom.

Queen Vashti had dishonoured the king and his authority, and she was banished from his presence. A decree was issued which had implications for every household in the empire. The Persians were proud of their laws and no important decision could ever be challenged; no decree issued could ever be revoked— it was final.

The command of an earthly king resulted in a negative response. In contrast, we read in John's Gospel chapter 4 of how Jesus spoke with authority to the woman at the well.[3] A command that came with spiritual wisdom, releasing her into true freedom and bringing salvation to the people of Samaria.

Consequences always follow disobedience to authority. In the beginning, man was banished from the presence of God through disobedience, and God set about a redemptive plan. Man, who was now denied access, would again enter the king's presence once that plan was fulfilled.

Moses felt inadequate when called by God, and tried to say no. Jonah said no but eventually had to yield to God's call. Mary said yes. God has a plan and purpose that will stand, and he leaves us a choice as to whether we will be a part of it.

---

[3] John 4:7-26

Meanwhile, the turn of events in Susa enabled those called to be instruments in God's plan and purposes to take their positions.

QUESTIONS

1.   **Esther 1:1-12, Psalm 45:10-11**
      Describe the opening scene. Who is King Xerxes?

      Why did Xerxes summon the queen?

How else might Vashti have responded? What would you have done?

How might this scene be viewed in today's society?

2. How do you respond to authority?

What do you do when our King calls? What do we forfeit when we refuse to obey our King's command?

Esther CHAPTER TWO

Preparation for the King

'The king's heart is in the hand of the Lord.'[4]

*Her background
as an adopted
child did not stop
her being chosen*

"Then let the girl who pleases the king be queen instead of Vashti."[5]

In time, it was proposed that a new queen be found. The king gave the order and the search began.

Many of the Jews exiled from the Davidic kingdom were living in the citadel of Susa. Amongst them was a Benjamite named Mordecai with his adopted daughter Hadassah, a Jewish orphan also known as Esther. The edict was proclaimed and many girls gathered in Susa to be taken to the king's palace.

Esther was also taken and set aside for a year to be subject to the required beauty treatments, her true identity remaining a secret. Esther would learn how to enter the king's presence, approach him and know what pleased him. With wisdom she followed the instructions of Hegai, one who knew the king better than she did.

---

[4] Proverbs 21:1
[5] Esther 2.4

ESTHER
For such a time as this

Esther would emerge as a woman of dignity, with a reverent fear of God instilled as a part of her upbringing and experiences. She learnt to trust, love and walk in obedience, and won the approval of the king.

She entered a year of refining, turning from what had been to what lay ahead, her desire only for the king. The doors of the palace closed to the outside world; no distractions as Esther prepared herself in the king's palace.

'Before a girl's turn came . . . twelve months of beauty treatments . . . six months with oil . . . six with perfumes.'[6]

Esther's first six months of preparation would leave her in a place where she would give herself completely, ready and prepared for entering the king's service. There would be consequences, for once she went to the king she would remain there. She would be available to no other man, even if the king no longer required her presence. Hers was a purpose beyond self: death to her own dreams, hopes and aspirations; no self-ambition. Esther had to give herself completely.

Then followed six months of being bathed in fragrances daily. No smell of the flesh or the world would remain.

---

[6] Esther 2:12

Included in the first six months of preparation was oil of myrrh. Myrrh was one of the ingredients in the holy anointing oil used in the tabernacle. An aromatic gum from the bark of balsam trees found in Ethiopia, Arabia and India, it had various uses in ancient times. It served to perfume the royal nuptial robes, and as an alluring feminine perfume.[7] The magi brought it to Jesus.[8] When mixed with wine it was used for pain relief.[9] After his crucifixion, myrrh was applied to Jesus' body.[10] Its purpose for Esther was to prepare her heart and stir her desire for the king.

Esther's approach was not about who she was, but about who the king was. Her background as an adopted child did not stop her being chosen, and indeed chosen to be used by God.

This nation of Israel had once been exiled, crying out in Egypt. In Eden, mankind had been exiled from the presence of God. As told by the prophet Isaiah, God was at work through the Persian dynasty, and so the choosing of a new bride by Xerxes—a young woman who was willing to serve—was part of God's sovereign plan and purpose.[11]

Meanwhile, Esther's cousin Mordecai remained watchful. He sat in the king's gate as one who held a

---

[7] Psalm 45:8, Song of Songs 5:5, Proverbs 7:17
[8] Matthew 2:11
[9] Mark 15:23
[10] John 19:39-40
[11] Isaiah 45:1-3

notable position in the empire. During this time, he played a significant role in the prevention of an attempt to assassinate the king.

As time passed, Esther was established as queen and the king gave a great banquet in her honour. A royal bride before her king, just as we are before our King, offering all of our worship to him. Worship in the presence of the Lord is our beauty treatment, for then we reflect and display his glory. A living sacrifice prepared for service to the King.

Late one December evening some years ago, I found myself unable to sleep and knew that God wanted to speak. There began what came to be known to those close to me as my 'Esther year', and it is upon this experience that much of this course is based. God spoke through the life of Esther about his call on my life; and through her relationship with the king, about my relationship with him. It was a year of preparation for the next phase of my walk with the Lord. A time to seek the Lord, humble myself and pray, so that the inner beauty of God would come forth in the months to follow.

Such a transformation in our lives is birthed in the place of prayer. Jesus submitted completely to the will of the Father in Gethsemane. In the place of prayer, we die to our own will and yield to his. As we lean on him and focus on him, then the change is from the inside out. We begin to reflect his beauty; there is an increase of clarity, wisdom, purpose and direction in our lives. We become more accustomed to him—to his voice, his moulding of our character—with an increased desire to enter his presence.

QUESTIONS

3. **Esther 2:8-18, Psalm 45:8-15**
    Describe the details of Esther's year of preparation. How did she prepare herself to approach the king?

4. **Ephesians 5:25-32, Romans 12:1-2, Revelation 19:6-8**
    (See **Ezekiel 16:9-5** for additional reading.)
    How should the bride of Christ make herself beautiful? How has God been preparing you?

ESTHER
For such a time as this

5.   **Luke 11:1-2; Psalm 100**
      How do you enter his presence? Why should you
      enter this way?

Esther CHAPTER THREE

Jews under threat

Enter Haman, who represents an historical enemy of the Jews.

Haman's ancestors are believed to be the Amalekites.[12] The Israelites were attacked by them following the exodus from Egypt, and later God instructed his people to 'blot them out'[13] —an instruction pursued by Saul, though not in its entirety.[14]

Following Haman's recent promotion, all officials were commanded to kneel before him. Mordecai was present amongst the royal officials, due to his own position of responsibility. He refused to kneel to Haman. To refuse to kneel before a higher official within the empire took great boldness on Mordecai's part. His refusal exposed Haman's deep-rooted hatred of the Jewish people. So Haman devised a plot to kill not only Mordecai, but the entire Jewish nation.

As the Jews prepared to celebrate the Passover, Haman stood before the king and raised his concern regarding 'a certain people', taking care not to

---

[12] Genesis 14:7, Exodus 17:8
[13] Deuteronomy 25:17-19
[14] 1 Samuel 15

mention those people specifically by name.[15] Haman's intention was to persuade the king to have the nation annihilated.

The enemy spoke as is customary: through a lie, deception or manipulation of the truth, seeking to undermine authority and gain control. For whilst it is true that the Jews did have their own customs and laws, these laws included being obedient to the ruling authority whilst in exile. God had commanded this at the time of the dispersion which had come as a consequence of their disobedience.[16]

As a result of this deception, the king's signet ring was now on the hand of Haman. Haman could now issue orders to destroy all the Jews in every province.

Haman promised the king that, in return for the annihilation decree, a huge amount of silver would be paid into the royal treasury—two thirds of the empire's annual income! (The coming Messiah would have a silver price of around half of a labourer's annual income.)

King Xerxes chose to have no part in the money, or — completely unaware of who exactly they were—the welfare of the people under threat. Likewise, Pilate would want no part in Jesus' death. And yet both leaders gave their assent to the execution.

---

[15] Esther 3:8-9
[16] Jeremiah 29:7

ESTHER
For such a time as this

We are continually faced with decisions that challenge our moral and spiritual integrity. In these circumstances God can sometimes seem to be silent or uninvolved; and yet the truth is that God sees and is sovereign, and his timing is perfect.

Haman's intent to annihilate the whole nation wouldn't be the last throughout history. The significance here is the redemptive plan of God.

Would such a plot against God's people be left unchallenged?

QUESTIONS

6.   **Esther 3:2-4**
     What sort of man was Mordecai?

7.   **Ezra 4:6, 2 Chronicles 16: 9, 2 Peter 3: 8-9**
     What examples can you give, throughout biblical
     history and beyond, of opposition and plots to kill the
     Jews?

     God is sovereign. Does anything escape his eye?

     How can you apply these verses to your own life at
     this point?

ESTHER
For such a time as this

Where do you need to be patient, trusting that in the proper time God will act according to his will and purpose?

ESTHER
For such a time as this

ESTHER CHAPTER FOUR

'For such a time as this'—a divine call and purpose

As God's chosen people, we are to live connected to the eternal perspective

We read here of Mordecai, a man of high position and integrity, not ashamed to declare publicly the heart of God for his people.

The edict to destroy the Jews came almost five years into Esther's role as queen. It would take another year to execute. Now Esther was required by her cousin to recognise the call of God and use her position of authority. Here before her stood the salvation of her people, or the very real possibility of her own death—unless the king extended the gold sceptre.

'. . . because you are in the king's house'[17]

A month had passed since Esther had last been in the presence of the king. She had a choice to make. Her status had elevated her to a position beyond that which she could have imagined. However, her protection did not rest in her position. Instead, it would come through her faith expressed in action and in her intercession.

---

[17] Esther 4:13

ESTHER
For such a time as this

Mordecai had challenged Esther not simply to sit in the place of luxury in the king's house, but to be ready to fulfil her call and purpose. A hungry orphan who had become a queen with plenty, she was reminded by Mordecai of where she had come from.

'I gave my life to Jesus' is an all too familiar testimony, yet the struggle to do his will above our own is very real. God has deposited vision and purpose in each one of us, though it comes at a cost to our flesh. In our western society, the challenge presents itself perhaps very differently from the open persecution and cost borne by our brothers and sisters in countries such as China, India and parts of Africa.

You too have a royal position in which you are seated, but the reality of the call is not to be ignored or forgotten whilst the riches of the kingdom are enjoyed. Jesus knew his call and the time when the hour had come.[18]

It was whilst Esther was serving the king that the plot regarding the Jews came to her attention. We are to remain faithful in what we are tasked to do until the word of the Lord comes—just as we see many times in the Old Testament, when the word came to the prophet or man of God. For Esther, it was time to forego the luxury of palace life—just as Daniel, another Jewish exile, did. When taken captive to Babylon, Daniel refused to partake of the royal food,

---

[18] John 12:23-26; 18:37

and later continued to pray three times a day even after it was forbidden and carried a death penalty.[19]

As God's chosen people, we are to live connected to the eternal perspective. That is, 'living for the line and not the dot', as I once heard it put, meaning not only for the here and now. So, we invest our dot in the line for an impact that goes beyond our mortal years.

The enemy issued a decree of death. The people of God gathered to fast and pray for three days.

God's will, will be done.

The shift came through prayer and fasting

There are times to be set aside and seek the Lord's will and intervention. In such times we discover an increased sensitivity to his will and not our own—a strengthening of the 'inner man'.

As Esther and her maids fasted and prayed, a supernatural shift took place, enabling the preparation for God's purpose to be fulfilled in and through her.

A similar process occurred some years later when Nehemiah, engaged as cupbearer to the Persian king

---

[19] Daniel 1:8, 6:10

Artaxerxes, was moved to pray for his people in Jerusalem and seek the king's permission to go and help them. Nehemiah thought not only of his own status and career, but for 'such a time as this'. Again, the shift came through prayer and fasting. For we do not seek to do in our own strength that which will be accomplished by God's Spirit. To seek him first is to clarify the strategy and open doors supernaturally. The cost is to the flesh. Will we die to it?

QUESTIONS

8. What similarities do you see between the call of Esther and that of Nehemiah and Daniel? (See **Nehemiah 1:2-10, Daniel 1:1 – 2:14-28** for further reading).

9. **Ephesians 2:6-10 and 3:20, Colossians 1:9-12,
    1 Peter 2:9-10, Isaiah 62:1**
    What do these verses tell us about God's sovereignty
    and our responsibility? Are we simply secure because
    we dwell in his house, or do we need to exercise
    individual responsibility?

    What is your position of influence and how will you
    use it?

10. **Matthew 26:36-45, Luke 22:39-46, Galatians 2:20**
    How does Esther's experience compare with that of
    Jesus in Gethsemane?

ESTHER
For such a time as this

Consider your own experiences and identify any time like this in your own life.

11. **Esther 4:12-14**

Who are the spiritual brothers/sisters who challenge you, as Mordecai challenged Esther?

ESTHER CHAPTERS FIVE AND SIX

Entering the King's presence

'Let us then approach the throne of grace with confidence.'[20]

Esther found favour before the king because she knew how to approach him

After those three days, Esther put on her royal robes, ready to approach the king's throne. We read that when he saw her standing in the court, he was pleased with her. The king, favourably disposed towards Esther, extended the golden sceptre when she entered without being summoned—in contrast to her predecessor, Vashti, who had refused to come when called.

Esther approached boldly, confident due to having sought the Lord, and so she entered the king's presence on the third day. What had taken place during those three days? God had given her the strategy to overcome the enemy, and she now knew her call and purpose. She stood in position, having done all—now God would do his part. For she was now submitted to the will of God, ready to cooperate with him in his plan for his people.

Esther wore a robe, which speaks of authority, position and favour. Later, we will see Mordecai with

---

[20] Hebrews 4:16

such a robe—a display symbolising honour, stature and the king's power.

Esther found favour before the king because she knew how to approach him. She did it right; she had the strategy—a banquet invitation. So the king and Haman attended the prepared banquet that very day.

It is interesting to see Esther's careful and measured approach. There was no hurry. Therein lies the wisdom of God: the apparent delay to voice her request left room for God to work. Neither did she allow herself to be distracted by the king's extremely generous offer of half his kingdom. Rather, she remained focused on the call.

God is sovereign

Esther's guests left the banquet with very different responses. We read that Haman left that day 'happy and in high spirits', then in the next moment filled with rage when Mordecai failed to acknowledge his presence once again. With some encouragement from his wife and friends, he ordered the execution tower to be built, ready for the Jew who would not bow.

The king, on the other hand, found himself troubled and unable to sleep. His sleepless night led to the uncovering of the truth about the earlier assassination attempt which Mordecai had reported.

As a result of these two very different reactions following a banquet, a series of events unfolded marking the beginning of God's plan to save his people.

'He who humbles himself...' [21] These are the words that Jesus used to conclude a parable as he observed a Pharisee's guests picking places of honour at the table.

It was left to Haman to decide how to express the king's gratitude to the man who had prevented his death. Haman's suggestion, with its selfish and hidden motive, pleased the king. The man who walked with humility would indeed wear the royal garment. To Haman's complete dismay, he was instructed to honour Mordecai.

Remember, the robe was a display of honour—and to be given the privilege of wearing the king's robe was a significant and unique sign of his favour. It would be a message to others that this man carried the royal authority in a special way.

God does it

Approaching the King of kings is for us now a great joy and privilege

Approaching the King of kings is for us now a great joy and privilege. No fear of death; only the hope of salvation and acceptance because of the precious blood of Jesus.[22]

---

[21] Luke 14:7-11, Proverbs 3:34, James 4:6
[22] Hebrews 4:16

Know that we enter because of the blood. He has clothed us in royal robes of righteousness. God sees us through the blood of the Lamb and is pleased with us. Standing in the robe of righteousness and because of Jesus, the sceptre of the One who sits on the throne is extended to us. Hallelujah!

Many of us have sung, 'In royal robes I don't deserve, I live to serve your majesty.'[23] The robe is for serving his majesty here in the kingdom of God.

The strategy for service must come from his majesty, the commander-in-chief. The battle plan is laid out and we must allow his wisdom to speak in the secret place.

We need to cooperate with his plan and trust him. Joseph, Daniel and others were used by God in the midst of their natural circumstances to bring about his supernatural purpose. Rest assured that God is sovereign and his timing is perfect! In these examples of men and women partnering with God, we see the change of the course of their lives and their nation.

You see, God always vindicates. The psalmists and the prophet Isaiah wrote often that no one whose hope was in the Lord would be put to shame. Though the enemy wants your downfall, the King has prepared a special place for you and given you a robe to wear.

---

[23] Song by Jarrod Cooper

QUESTIONS

12. **Esther 5:1-5**
How did Esther present herself to the king?

13. **Isaiah 52:1-2, 61:10, Revelation 19:5-9**
Describe your robe.

14. **Psalm 34:4-5, Psalm 127:5, Isaiah 28:16**
What do you need to trust the Lord for?

15. **Esther 5:6**
    This offer of instant promotion was often made by kings and rulers. (See **Daniel 5:13-16, Mark 6:21-23, Luke 4:5-8** for further reading)

    What disguise does temptation wear when it comes to you?

16. **John 14:12-14, Hebrews 4:14-16**
    What does Jesus offer us?

Esther CHAPTER SEVEN

Anything you ask

You prepare a table before me in the presence of my enemies.[24]

Once again, the king and Haman joined Esther to dine. It would seem that the king had not tired of these invitations, but was keen to know what troubled Esther as she sat in his presence. He again made a very generous offer, if in her view the role of queen was not enough.

Esther did not shortcut the strategy that came through seeking the Lord

Anything you ask according to his will. The king was willing to give up to half the kingdom. For Esther, the banquet was spread in the presence of her enemy as she ate with the king. For Haman, it was indeed a great honour to be invited to the banquet, for who else had been invited to dine with the king and queen?

Haman relished this invitation, but unfortunately it was one that he had completely misunderstood.

It was at this point that Esther had to expose both her true identity and Haman's plot, using the wisdom that

---

[24] Psalm 23:5

had come during that time of fasting. Godly wisdom that brought about a rapid turn of events.

So Mordecai was vindicated. Esther revealed the plot, and two charges now stood against Haman.

Haman the enemy now found himself at the feet of a Jewish woman, pleading for his life—before he met his end on the very gallows he had built.

Deliverance! Esther did not shortcut the strategy that came through seeking the Lord, to get the end result, but rather she rested in the sovereignty of God. She pressed through before the king for the breakthrough, and beyond into complete victory.

Mordecai's response to Haman's threat reminds us that we need to stand firm in the face of the accuser. What did God require of Esther and her cousin? Obedience to the call for 'such a time as this'. Their willingness to surrender to his purpose opened the way to victory over the enemy, and to salvation for the Jewish nation.

Jesus' death allows us the full rights of the kingdom of God, and we enter into its richness as we yield to him. Moreover, when we approach him we must know that there is mercy and grace readily available to us.[25] Jesus has already defeated the enemy—the accuser of the brethren—and at the name of Jesus now every

---

[25] Hebrews 4.16

ESTHER
For such a time as this

knee will bow. God is ready to use us if we will allow
him.

QUESTIONS

17. **Psalm 7**
How does this psalm apply in Esther and her nation's
situation? Do you see its application in your life?

18. **Philippians 2:5-18, Revelation 12:10-11**
Are you able to stand in your place in obedience? Is
there any other name than Jesus that can stand? What
situation in your life needs to bow at the name of
Jesus?

19. According to **Ephesians 1** and **Colossians 1,** what has the Father given you in Christ?

20. **Psalm 42:5-11**
Do you think Esther's hope was in King Xerxes alone? Explain. Where should we place our hope?

21. **Luke 11:5-10**
In the Amplified Version of the Bible, this passage speaks of the 'shameless persistence and insistence' of the friend who kept asking. See also the parable of the persistent widow in Luke 18:1-8. What is God asking of you that requires patient endurance, faith and trust?

22. **Psalm 23:4-6**

    Can you believe and trust now that the Good
    Shepherd will lead you through to victory?

ESTHER CHAPTERS EIGHT TO NINE

The gold sceptre

'The king extended the gold sceptre . . . and she arose and stood before him.'[26]

Entreat the Lord and never give up until the victory is complete

It is recorded that in ancient times the property of a traitor reverted to the crown. So all that had belonged to Haman was now in the hands of Esther. That very day, Mordecai was acknowledged as Esther's blood relative and received the signet ring that had once belonged to Haman. He left the king's presence wearing royal robes! He left changed, for now he carried a new level of authority with higher rank and status.

Haman's ancestral line was probably that of the Amalekites, a nation that God had commanded the Israelites—led by Saul the Benjamite—to annihilate completely. Centuries later, Mordecai was the Benjamite who remembered.

Esther was safe and so was her cousin, but what of their nation?

Entreat the Lord and never give up until the victory is complete and the enemy's influence driven out.

---

[26] Esther 8:4

ESTHER
For such a time as this

Esther had sought the Lord and received strength from him alone—strength to stand before Xerxes, the king of the empire, and against her enemy, Haman.

The law that stood against Esther and her people could not be revoked, because any decree issued in Persia at that time was final; the death sentence had been issued. The dilemma facing Xerxes recalls that of his father Darius who was deceived into commanding the death of Daniel.[27] God honoured Daniel's faith and saved him from the lions.

Esther wept and pleaded with the king. She was able to prevail on behalf of her people. A new decree was written, which countered the one issued by Haman. The new edict, sealed by Mordecai with the king's signet ring, gave the Jews the right to defend themselves—against *any* enemy.

Mordecai left the king's presence with the king's decree, and Haman's wicked scheme was overturned. The Jews, now very much aware of the new edict, were filled with courage to stand and gain victory, under the new leadership instituted by the king. No one could stand against them, for this had always been God's sovereign promise as given to Abraham: 'I will bless those who bless you and whoever curses you I will curse.'[28]

---

[27] Daniel chapter 6
[28] Genesis 12:3

ESTHER
For such a time as this

The longstanding enemy of the Jews was defeated under the authority of the king, and the Jewish nation gained the support of all the officials in the Persian empire!

A day of joy and feasting followed—the feast of Purim. Mordecai distributed letters throughout the provinces, calling all Jews to mark the day according to Esther's decree. For sorrow had turned to joy and mourning to celebration.

QUESTIONS

23. **Esther 3:13, 8:7-8,11, 1 Samuel 15:1-9**
    Compare:
    a) Mordecai's battle strategy with Saul's in 1 Samuel 15:1-9, and
    b) Haman's edict in chapter 3:13 with Mordecai's edict and the king's words in chapter 8:7-8,11.

24. **Luke 15:21-24 and read Isaiah 61:10 again**
     Remind yourself of what God has done for you in
     Christ.

25. What is available to us because of the seal of the Holy
     Spirit **(Ephesians 1:13)?**

26. **Esther 8:6, Genesis18:20-33, Daniel 9:1-19, 11:32**
     Are you ready to intercede for those who do not yet
     wear the royal robes nor have favourable access to
     the King's estate—his kingdom?

ESTHER
For such a time as this

27.   **Esther 8 :13-14, Psalm 103:19-22, Hebrews 1:14**
What picture do these verses give regarding the role
of the heavenly hosts?

28.   **Esther 8:16-17**
When faced with a challenge or adverse
circumstances, whose report will you believe? With
whom will you join rank?

29.   **Esther 9:5-10, Ephesians 6:10-18, 2 Corinthians
10:3-5, Psalm 91**
Who is our enemy? What is our position? How do we
fight?

C ONCLUSION

The new decree

'. . . pre-eminent among the Jews and held in high esteem.'[29]

Mordecai was now second in rank to the king. He now lived to serve the king in royal robes, bearing a crown, wherever he went.

We wear a robe of righteousness and we are to walk in it wherever we go

We must recognise that our position before our King is due to his grace, mercy and love. Let us boldly approach with reverence and awe, for it is a holy throne of grace and mercy.

The law of the Old Covenant has not been revoked; it has been fulfilled in Christ Jesus. The King of kings issued a new decree—the New Covenant—at the Passover meal before he went to the cross. It is sealed and ratified by the shedding of his blood. The sceptre is extended to us, and we kneel before the authority of the King in order to walk in his divine authority and share the privileges of his estate—his kingdom.[30]

We are to be sure and certain of the details of this New Covenant. We should not allow ourselves to be

---

[29] Esther 10:3
[30] John14:13, 16:23-24

overcome by the attack of the enemy, but rather we walk in the triumph of Jesus who has taken the keys of death and hell. He enables us to stand and avenge ourselves against enemy attack. We 'plunder hell and populate heaven' by the power of the Spirit.[31]

What was written in the king's name was made known; the couriers, who raced out on royal horses, a picture of the heavenly hosts who go out at God's command.

So, when leaving the King's presence we leave assured that he has answered, aware of our position and the royal robes that we wear! We leave accepted, and with authority in the name of King Jesus. This is our inheritance and salvation.

We wear a robe of righteousness and we are to walk in it wherever we go. Living as God intended; leading others to him, as the reverent fear of God and the joy of salvation are displayed in and through our lives.

Consider what that means for you and me: the seal of the Holy Spirit made possible through the blood of Jesus.[32] The-blood that has rescued us from death.

Are we known to the enemy? Are we scared of him, or does he fear us as a people who know their position and who they are?

---

[31] See 'Plundering Hell To Populate Heaven: Reinhard Bonnke's Vision', a book by Ron Steele, published by Dove Christian Books.
[32] Ephesians 1:13

ESTHER
For such a time as this

As I write this chapter, the Jewish nation is about to begin the celebration of Purim held on the fourteenth of Adar, which is early March. It is the day still marked to commemorate the nation's miraculous salvation.

It bears emphasising once again that in the book of Esther the name of the Lord is never mentioned. Yet his hand in this miracle is clear for those who can see it—almost disguised through a course of natural events.

'For we are God's workmanship, created in Christ Jesus to do good works, which God prepared in advance for us to do.'[33]

At the beginning of the story, Queen Vashti—the most important woman of the harem—was deposed. The way was opened for a Jewish orphan girl to be raised up as queen, though her identity was not revealed at that time.

Esther was indeed called 'for such a time as this', positioned for noble purposes far higher than that of Queen to King Xerxes. The call of God on her life required boldness and courage, and it could not be fulfilled in her own strength. Following the godly counsel of her relative, she had to rely fully on God.

The Saviour has made the way for us. God has extended to us the royal sceptre, prepared a feast for

---

[33] Ephesians 2:10

us, and called us to his banqueting table for his purposes—to see his kingdom come and his will be done.

Esther did not sit and dwell upon her natural life status, her worth or her life's lot as an orphan. Rather, she boldly embraced the future and the opportunity that was laid out before her.

There are many other examples in scripture of women called 'for such a time as this'. They would lay hold of the prophetic vision and be ready, whether their time was equal to an hour, a day, a year or a lifetime. There are many men and women in the Bible who remain unknown—not mentioned by name, that is—who had their moment to go for God. There have been many since and there are many today—those whom the Lord our God calls, irrespective of rank, race or gender.

The work of God will be done. Will you be a part of it for his glory?

You are called and positioned for such a time as this.

QUESTIONS

30. **Jeremiah 31:11-14, Psalm 30:11-12 and Isaiah 61:1-3.**
     Recount the day when you gained relief from the enemy, when your sorrow turned to joy and mourning into celebration.

     Offer up a prayer of thanksgiving and praise for that day.

31. **Review**
     The banquet table is spread (see the Appendix). What does that mean for you now?

ESTHER
For such a time as this

Are you willing to be used?

Is your life devoted to his service?

APPENDIX

The King's banquet

The following is an extract from my journal. It was written during the period I called my 'Esther year'.

Empty yourself of self, and come and eat of his table—of what he has prepared for you

He has brought me to his banqueting table, to the banquet of love—a love feast spread.

The table is laden with everything you need. There is a plate of self-control, plates of peace, healing, love, joy . . . and you are invited to eat of the banquet, which everyone does, though not in a greedy way. All eat, but all eyes are fixed; all attention is on the King. All are enthralled by his beauty and cannot take their eyes off him. All are so honoured to be invited to sit at the table that they eat carefully, slowly.

Then the King stands and visits each guest in turn. asking if they are enjoying the banquet and how they are.

I tell him how busy my days are—so many things in my life.

He says to me, "Your heart is full of so many desires; each one has its place in time." He shows me how to order them and reminds me that I don't need to try to live my whole life in one day!

ESTHER
For such a time as this

I eat of self-control. I need his wisdom not always to say yes or respond to every desire of my heart immediately. To focus on him and remain true to the call he has given.

'To come to the banquet, you cannot come full,' he says. 'For if you know that you are invited to a feast, will you eat your fill before you come? No, you will come hungry, ready to eat what is there.'

Empty yourself of self, and come and eat of his table—of what he has prepared for you.

This is the best way to enjoy the banquet.

The banquet table is laden with everything the King has to offer. What does he offer you? What is it you need at this time? You are invited to come and eat.

A feast laden with everything you need. You are invited to eat and be satisfied in His presence with the food he gives.

What will you take from the heavenly banquet?

ESTHER
For such a time as this

He has taken me to the banquet hall and his banner
over me is love (Song of Songs 2:4)

GOING DEEPER

The following resources were used in the preparation of this study, and are recommended for those who wish to study the book of Esther further.

1. **Iran In the Bible: The Forgotten Story**

   A 28-minute film, directed by Jeff Baxter. Available at the time of printing as a DVD, and on Amazon Prime Video.

2. **Commentary on Esther**

   An audio commentary on the book of Esther by John McKay. Available at no charge at **www.thewayofthespirit.com/project/esther/**

3. **www.chabad.org**

   A source of Jewish practice, culture and values.

THE WAY OF THE SPIRIT

The Way of The Spirit has a series of Bible reading and study programmes, giving a guide to the whole Bible as seen through the activity and experience of the Holy Spirit.

HOME AND FURTHER STUDY COURSES

Various levels of study and training are available, including short Bible Reading courses similar to this one, and the full-length Reading Course that covers the whole Bible in four units.

Discipleship training and Bible teacher training courses are available either via Zoom or through attending a series of short residential schools. Both options include mentored training that you can take in local groups and seminars.

For more information, email **resources@thewayofthespirit.com**, or go to **www.thewayofthespirit.com/training_overview/**